G. RUGER DONOHO

A Painter's Path

G. RUGER DONOHO

A Painter's Path

René Paul Barilleaux and Victoria J. Beck
Introductory Essay by Victoria J. Beck

Mississippi Museum of Art
in association with
University Press of Mississippi

G. Ruger Donoho: A Painter's Path is supported by Deposit Guaranty National Bank; Mrs. Thomas M. Hederman, Jr.; the Thomas M. Hederman, Jr. Fund; and the National Endowment for the Arts, a federal agency.

Exhibition organized by René Paul Barilleaux, Director of Exhibitions and Collections/Chief Curator, Mississippi Museum of Art and Victoria J. Beck.

Kathryn Howarth Ryan, Editor
Beth Warren Turnage, Assistant Curator/Registrar

Exhibition Schedule

Mississippi Museum of Art
Jackson, Mississippi
September 8 - November 4, 1995
Heckscher Museum
Huntington, New York
December 9, 1995 - February 4, 1996
Greenville County Museum of Art
Greenville, South Carolina
April 17 - June 23, 1996

Manufactured in U.S.A.
Designed by John A. Langston
Drawing on title page: *North West Knoll*

Mississippi Museum of Art
201 East Pascagoula Street
Jackson, Mississippi 39201

Library of Congress Cataloging-in-Publication Data

Barilleaux, René Paul.

G. Ruger Donoho : a painter's path / René Paul Barilleaux and Victoria J. Beck; introductory essay by Victoria J. Beck.

p. cm.

Catalog of an exhibition held at the Mississippi Museum of Art, Sept. 8-Nov. 4, 1995; Heckscher Museum, Huntington, N.Y., Dec. 9, 1995-Feb. 4, 1996; and Greenville County Museum of Art, Greenville, S.C., Apr. 17-June 23, 1996.

Includes bibliographical references.

ISBN 0-87805-797-8 (cloth : acid-free paper). — ISBN 0-87805-798-6 (pbk. : acid-free paper)

1. Donoho, Gaines Ruger, 1857-1916—Exhibitions. I. Donoho, Gaines Ruger, 1857-1916. II. Beck, Victoria J. III. Mississippi Museum of Art. IV. Heckscher Museum. V. Greenville County Museum of Art.

N6537.D585A4 1995

759.13—dc20 95-13391

CIP

British Library Cataloging-in-Publication data available

Contents

Director's Foreword

Great artists have been born and nurtured in Mississippi, most notably in literature and music. Mississippi's visual artists have a more elusive history. Few have garnered their reputations nationally.

It is fitting that the Mississippi Museum of Art present and commemorate the artistic talents native to Mississippi, thus providing Mississippians with greater knowledge and pride of their own artistic heritage.

It is our objective and great pleasure to undertake the first comprehensive exhibition and publication commemorating the artistic achievements of Gaines Ruger Donoho. Born in 1857 in Church Hill, Mississippi, Donoho became one of America's foremost Impressionist painters and a pioneer of the East Hampton, New York, artist community.

In this catalog the museum documents Donoho's work and evaluates his place in American art. The exhibition of over thirty paintings and drawings will be shown in Jackson then tour nationally through 1996.

With much gratitude, the Mississippi Museum of Art wishes to acknowledge the diligence, support, commitment and hard work of many individuals and institutions that have contributed to the creation of this project. Early support from the National Endowment for the Arts established the groundwork for this exhibition. M.P. Naud of Hirschl & Adler Galleries assisted in locating many of Donoho's works.

Most notably, Dr. Victoria J. Beck has directed this project with careful research, evaluation and documentation. She has given curatorial form to this exhibition, working along with the museum's Chief Curator, René Paul Barilleaux; Assistant Curator/Registrar, Beth Warren Turnage; and Preparators L.C. Tucker, Jr. and Melvin Johnson.

We wish to thank the University Press of Mississippi for their interest in this project, with special thanks to Dr. Richard M. Abel, Director; JoAnne Prichard, Executive Editor; John A. Langston, Design and Production Manager; and Ginger Tucker, Managing Editor. We also wish to thank Kathryn Howarth Ryan who provided editorial assistance throughout the development of this work.

We are greatly indebted to the lenders who have provided Donoho's works and to the exhibition's lead sponsors, Deposit Guaranty National Bank; Mrs. Thomas M. Hederman, Jr.; the Thomas M. Hederman, Jr. Fund; and the National Endowment for the Arts for their support of the exhibition and publication. Without the interest and generosity of these contributors, this exhibition and publication would not have been possible.

Linda S. Sullivan
Executive Director

Preface

It is about one hundred years since G. Ruger Donoho lived and worked in East Hampton on Long Island, New York. It has also been over one hundred years since he was born here in Mississippi or rendered the countryside of France in his drawings and paintings. Within the intervening century, this important American artist and his works have been largely overshadowed by more popular artists and nearly forgotten by art history. This exhibition, the first to survey the full range of Donoho's art, traces it from interpretations of rural France to impressions of the American East Coast landscape. The majority of these works, gathered from numerous public and private collections, are exhibited together for the first time.

As the largest art museum in Mississippi, an important aspect of the Mississippi Museum of Art's mission is to collect, preserve and exhibit the work of artists native to the state. The museum strives to strengthen the appreciation of the region's past and present artists within a greater national and international context. While the mission centers largely on artists working in this century—Walter Anderson, Marie Hull, William Hollingsworth and William Dunlap, for example—*G. Ruger Donoho: A Painter's Path* adds a significant historical contribution to the museum's efforts. The presentation of the exhibition in Huntington, Long Island, and in Greenville, South Carolina, following its Jackson premier enhances the project in terms of the numbers of viewers, but also broadens the understanding of Donoho's work and brings an awareness of his roots in the Deep South to audiences in areas where he is better known.

In the following essay, Dr. Victoria J. Beck reconstructs Donoho's biography and explores his career as an artist within the larger history of late nineteenth-century American art. She often incorporates work included in this exhibition in telling Donoho's life story. Dr. Beck painstakingly assembles primary material from numerous, diverse sources which she interweaves with the artistic revolutions of Donoho's historical period. In many instances, this catalogue gathers and presents biographical material previously unavailable for research and study. The accompanying chronology and bibliography provide further direction to those interested in a deeper investigation of Donoho's art. The checklist of works, selection of color images and several black and white photographs and facsimiles strengthen the overall documentary nature of this catalogue. It is important to acknowledge that the inspiration for all of these efforts lies in the paintings and drawings of G. Ruger Donoho.

René Paul Barilleaux
Director of Exhibitions
and Collections/Chief Curator

Acknowledgments

Many individuals and institutions assisted in the interesting and pleasurable endeavor of bringing to light the prodigious talent of Gaines Ruger Donoho. Individuals I would like to thank for facilitating my research in the most helpful and generous way include Judy Throm of Reference Services at the Archives of American Art, Smithsonian Institution; Lawrence Campbell from the Art Students League; and Janice Lurie, librarian at the Albright-Knox Art Gallery. I must also acknowledge the aid of the staffs at The New York Public Library; the Emerson Institute, Washington, D.C.; and the Washington Historical Society. Dorothy T. King of the East Hampton Library deserves special mention for sharing with me her considerable knowledge of East Hampton's history. Heartfelt gratitude is owed Patricia Sinclair Sliwienski for her help in exploring Donoho's Long Island years. At the beginning of this project, Ronald Pisano kindly offered suggestions and leads.

With respect to Donoho's works, I wish to thank M.P. Naud of the Hirschl & Adler Galleries for her expert assistance; Barbara Dayer Gallati, Associate Curator of American Painting and Sculpture at The Brooklyn Museum; H. Barbara Weinberg, Curator of American Painting and Sculpture at The Metropolitan Museum of Art; Elaine Cobos, Curator at The Museums at Stony Brook; Judy Larson, Curator of American Painting at the High Museum of Art; Alicia Longwell, Registrar at The Parrish Art Museum; and Martha R. Severens, Curator at the Greenville County Museum of Art. It is with great appreciation that I thank Dan Flavin, James J. Shields and Frederick Hill for the opportunity to examine and appreciate Donoho's works in the most cordial and pleasant surroundings. I am also grateful to Prudence Fairweather for her always gracious assistance.

I wish to thank René Paul Barilleaux, Director of Exhibitions and Collections/Chief Curator at the Mississippi Museum of Art, for inviting me to participate in this exhibition and for being such an intelligent and inspirational collaborator. Beth Warren Turnage, Assistant Curator/Registrar at the museum, gave invaluable and greatly appreciated help. I thank my editor, Kathryn Howarth Ryan, for her perceptive, professional advice. A special thanks to

James D. Newman for his research assistance and unflagging interest in this project. Finally, as always, much gratitude to Jean and Werner Beck for their encouragement and support.

Victoria J. Beck

Lenders to the Exhibition

Mr. and Mrs. Holmes S. Adams
Jackson, Mississippi

Art Gallery of Ontario
Toronto, Ontario, Canada

Dr. Nancy Burrow and
Dr. Kenneth Williams
Brandon, Mississippi

Mr. and Mrs. Charles E. Carmichael
Jackson, Mississippi

East Hampton Library
East Hampton, New York

Dan Flavin
Wainscott, New York

Greenville County Museum of Art
Greenville, South Carolina

High Museum of Art
Atlanta, Georgia

May and Frederick Hill
New York, New York

Mr. and Mrs. William Kehl
Greenville, South Carolina

The Metropolitan Museum of Art
New York, New York

Mr. and Mrs. Charles C. Mickel
Greenville, South Carolina

Mississippi Museum of Art
Jackson, Mississippi

Mr. and Mrs. Davenport Mosby
Jackson, Mississippi

The Museums at Stony Brook
Stony Brook, New York

National Museum of American Art,
Smithsonian Institution
Washington, D.C.

New Orleans Museum of Art
New Orleans, Louisiana

The Parrish Art Museum
Southampton, New York

James J. Shields
New York, New York

Mr. and Mrs. Harry M. Walker
Jackson, Mississippi

G. RUGER DONOHO

A Painter's Path

The Life and Art of Gaines Ruger Donoho

The friends, acquaintances and mentors who helped to shape the career of American painter Gaines Ruger Donoho include some of the most illustrious and eminent artists of the late nineteenth century. Over the course of a decade-long stay in France, he was associated with the leading lights of the French Academy—traditionalists such as Gustave-Rodolphe Boulanger, Jules-Joseph Lefebvre and Adolphe-William Bouguereau. Donoho also worked within the innovative milieu created by the Barbizon school and attracted critical admiration for his works from the French Symbolist Pierre Puvis de Chavannes and the American expatriate James McNeill Whistler.[1] His closest contemporaries were Childe Hassam, William Merritt Chase, Willard Metcalf, Robert Reid and Kenyon Cox, all artists of prominent stature within the canon of American art history. Donoho's relationships with these individuals and their works exercised a profound influence upon his stylistic development and the formal progression of his painting.

Donoho created highly distinctive landscape paintings which were ranked by art critics and exhibition juries among the best works produced by an American painter of his era. Unfortunately for the art historian wishing to construct an accurate and comprehensive account of the artist's life and art, Donoho, unlike his friends Hassam, Chase and John Carroll Beckwith, did not write about his views on art or artistic practice nor do his papers include even a personal diary. In addition, he spent the last twenty years of his life working in relative seclusion away from the major centers of the art world. If Donoho's name is not a standard reference in histories of nineteenth-century American art, the omission is largely due to his disinclination toward publicity during his lifetime, preferring, in the words of Hassam, to "pursue his calling in quiet and solitude."[2] However, despite Donoho's reticence and his reluctance to engage in self-promotional activities in order to further his career, his great talent is a matter of historical record in period reviews, exhibition notes and annals, the letters and journals of friends and acquaintances and, most significantly, in his sketchbooks and paintings. These primary sources provide the evidential basis for an historical account of Donoho's life and art—an account in which he emerges as an important participant in the movements which dominated the American art scene in the latter years of the nineteenth century.

G. Ruger Donoho began his life in a region remote from the cosmopolitan venues of the art world at a less than propitious moment in American history. He was born in Church Hill, Mississippi, on December 21, 1857.[3] His father was a prosperous plantation owner whose family had come to the Deep South from Virginia in the early part of the century.[4] Then, as now, Church Hill and the surrounding area of Jefferson County were agrarian territories divided into small farms and cotton plantations.[5] Fueled by slave labor, the plantations were largely self-sufficient with respect to manufacturing needs and the sole independent industry in Jefferson County was a tannery where leather goods were produced.[6] A private school may have existed, but education among wealthier land-owners was provided at home by private tutors. Donoho spent his first years in these pastoral and privileged circumstances. Because he was uprooted from this situation at a very young age, one can only speculate as to the depth of the impression of his experiences in Mississippi. It is possible that his adult preference for the countryside with respect to both the subjects found in his art and the rural environment in which he chose to reside were fostered by memories of his birthplace.

Donoho's childhood was severely disrupted by the onset of the Civil War in 1860. According to the artist's recollections, his father died in the early 1860s, although Donoho did not specify the cause of his death.[7] Faced with the escalation of the conflict and the impending defeat of the Confederacy, his mother, Julia Donoho, whom her son described as descended from "New England stock,"[8] determined to flee Mississippi and appealed to her northern relatives for help. In what must have been a dramatic rescue, a group of United States cavalrymen sent by Julia Donoho's cousin, General Thomas Howard Ruger,[9] arrived in Church Hill toward the end of the war and transported the artist and his mother to the relative safety of Vicksburg which was at that point under the control of Union forces. Donoho later related the tale of his flight to Hassam who remarked,

> *He described the coming of the United States cavalrymen (sent by his mother's relative, General Ruger) to his house early one morning and his mother and he riding away with them to Vicksburg, he up behind a trooper. He told that so well that you felt as if you had been there yourself.*[10]

Eventually mother and son made their way to Washington, D.C., where the artist remained until 1878. (It is likely that the Donoho family was living in Washington by the late 1860s as Donoho reported to Hassam that he grew up there. A directory of the District of Columbia from 1874 lists the residence of Julia Ruger Donoho as 1332 I Street, N.W.[11]) The details of his upbringing in the capital are sketchy but it is known that he attended the prestigious Emerson Institute, a preparatory school for young men where the artist's classmates included the two younger sons of President Ulysses S. Grant.[12] The Emerson Institute specialized in readying candidates for entrance to the service academies, notably the Naval Academy, the Coast Guard Academy and West Point.[13] Donoho's cousin, General Thomas Ruger, was superintendent of West Point throughout the seventies and it is possible that the future artist was being prepared for a military career. In keeping with the school's orientation, students were required to fulfill an academic program heavily weighted in favor of mathematics and the sciences. Mechanical drawing was a prerequisite for the successful completion of a degree and it is probable that the technical excellence of Donoho's draughtsmanship, a feature evident even in his student works, was facilitated by the early training he received at the Emerson Institute. Apparently not inclined toward military service, Donoho enrolled at the State Normal School in Millersville, Pennsylvania, in 1874 where he studied for two years.

Returning to Washington in 1876, he was employed by the Office of the United States Architect. His name appears in a city census taken in 1877 and is listed with an address and the designation "draughtsman" in the 1877 edition of *Boyd's Directory of the District of Columbia.*[14] A letter written by his mother and dated September 21, 1878, indicates that by this time Donoho had begun to study painting in earnest. On Donoho's behalf she wrote to the noted landscape painter

Jervis McEntee, whose sketch of Natural Bridge they had seen in Washington, asking that he accept her son as a pupil. She noted that Donoho had studied with "the best artists" in Washington who recommended him for his "decided talents." The letter also makes mention of Donoho's plan to attend classes at the National Academy of Design in New York the following winter after a summer and fall spent "sketching in oils in the Catskills." Whether or not Julia Donoho knew of McEntee's appointment as a teacher at the Academy is unclear since she expressed her desire that in addition to his classes Donoho should "spend part of the time" there working under "some eminent artist" and "master" by which she meant McEntee.[15]

There is no record of McEntee's response to Julia Donoho's request but by November 1878 Donoho had departed Washington for New York in order to study painting. In a surprising turn of events the aspiring young artist did not elect to pursue coursework at the National Academy of Design.[16] Instead, an application card bearing his name and a notation of the receipt of five dollars to cover the cost of tuition expenses for the year 1878-1879 offer proof of his enrollment at the newly formed Art Students League.[17]

This change of plans may have been motivated by Donoho's recognition of the contentious and precarious situation of the National Academy of Design in the 1870s.[18] Wracked by internal dissension and in financial difficulty, the Academy sharply curtailed its studio curriculum. In response, a group of angry and disappointed students under the leadership of Academy Professor Lemuel Wilmarth united to form an independent society of artists interested in the kind of training the Academy was no longer able to offer.[19] The group organized as an official body in 1875 as the Art Students League, the first student-run arts school in the United States. As Lois Fink and Joshua Taylor point out, the formation of the League was not motivated by ideological opposition to the philosophies and methodologies promoted by the National Academy but "solely by the immediate practical necessity of continuing with the serious study of art."[20] If the Academy could not guarantee the maintenance of a quality program, the League would strive to "meet the want thus occasioned."[21]

When Donoho arrived in New York in 1878, the Academy had begun to recover from its financial woes and to reinstate most of its studio classes. However, the troubles which plagued the Academy during the previous years were widely publicized by the press and engendered a fair amount of public hostility. To a newcomer eager to embark upon his studies, uncertainty regarding continuation of the Academy's studio schools may have made it seem a less than auspicious place to begin a career. It is also possible that Donoho, already an experienced draughtsman, did not want to invest either time or money in the Antique School courses which were required of every student at the National Academy of Design prior to the life sessions. As Julia Donoho stated in her letter to McEntee, he had "limited means," and the lower fees of the Art Students League in addition to their more flexible standards for admission to the life and painting courses might have made it an attractive alternative. Robert Swain Gifford, under whom Donoho studied in New York, was teaching at the Cooper Union School and may have directed him to the Art Students League. Donoho is listed as Gifford's pupil in the records of the Paris Salon for 1881 and 1882[22] and may have worked with him earlier in Washington.[23]

Donoho's teachers at the Art Students League were Walter Shirlaw, who led the composition classes, and William Merritt Chase, in painting and drawing. Both men were veterans of Wilhelm Leibl's studio at the Royal Academy in Munich. Chase's work in particular is characteristic of the Munich School in its Realist approach to portraiture and genre subjects and preference for rich, broadly brushed surfaces. As opposed to the precise, linear style demanded in the laborious mechanical drawing Donoho performed while working for the United States Architect, Shirlaw and Chase taught him the quick-sketch method in

FIGURE 1. *Old Ruins, Van Ness Place,* dated June 1879 in the artist's hand, graphite on paper. First known extant work by Donoho. Gaines Ruger Donoho Papers, Archives of American Art, Smithsonian Institution, Washington, D.C. Gift of John R. Hopkins.

which an artist draws very rapidly and freely in order to retain the immediate sensations of a given subject.[24] (Figure 1) (Ironically, Shirlaw and Chase's teachings were antithetical to the conservative style favored by Donoho's would-be mentor, the academician Jervis McEntee who had only contempt for pictures based upon "honest impressions of nature."[25]) Rather than undergoing a complete conversion to the quick-sketch manner, many of Donoho's finished drawings from the early 1880s reveal a synthesis of the competing drawing aesthetics. (Figures 2, 3 and 4) In *Forge, Fleury* (1880) and *Millet's House, Barbizon* (1880) for example, the overall compositions achieved in sections of furious cross-hatching appear spontaneously conceived. This spontaneity is especially evident in the natural elements which are represented with rapid lines and abundant masses of shading. But in both drawings, the architectural structures are carefully described with close attention to details such as the iron chimney caps of the forge and the wooden slats and dark metal hinges of the shutters and doors on the houses lining Millet's street.[26]

Donoho's tenure at the Art Students League was a brief one. The sites represented in *Forge, Fleury* and *Millet's House, Barbizon* were located in the French countryside and in fact Donoho embarked for France in 1879 seeking the opportunity to expand the scope of his training and experience. From a general historical standpoint, Donoho's decision to carry on his studies in France testifies to the widespread perception among mid-nineteenth-century American artists that no matter how inspired and original, American art was singularly lacking in what could be termed "pedigree."

The virtual exodus of young American painters to France in the post-Civil War period points to a shift in cultural perspective toward American art at this time. As several scholars have recently pointed out, American art prior to the War Between the States was valued for its freedom from servitude to moribund traditions. If American works were perceived as inferior in comparison to the technical virtuosity demonstrated in European art, this deficiency was mitigated by the vitality and originality of styles unhampered by a slavish devotion to the past. This viewpoint was profoundly altered with the introduction of Darwinian theory into nearly every field of intellectual endeavor in the mid-nineteenth century. As Fink posits, the recognition of Darwin's concept of life as evolutionary, when applied to the arts, meant that "Human cultural productions, like biological life forms, had

FIGURE 2. *Forge, Fleury,* 1880, graphite on paper, 10 ¼" x 13 ½". Collection of Mr. and Mrs. Davenport Mosby, Jackson, Mississippi.

FIGURE 3. *Millet's House, Barbizon,* 1880, graphite on paper, 10 ¼" x 13 ½". Collection of Dr. Nancy Burrow and Dr. Kenneth Williams, Brandon, Mississippi. Donoho lived in France from 1879 until 1887. Many drawings and paintings from these years attest to his passionate attraction to the rural areas surrounding Barbizon.

FIGURE 4.
Churchyard, c. 1881,
graphite on paper,
10 ¼" x 13 ½".
Collection of Mississippi Museum of Art, Jackson.
Gift of Gallery Guild.
1979.003.

origins in the past and required time to develop gradually through the ages."[27] The absence of a past, once the valorizing mark of American art, was perceived as a liability for native artists wishing to participate in the advancement of civilization. If works of art were to be judged and valued according to their place in an evolutionary chain, Europe, rich in an artistic history accrued over hundreds of centuries, seemed a logical place to go.

American art students in Paris desiring formal art instruction chose from among a variety of programs. The most popular was that offered by the government-sponsored École des Beaux-Arts.[28] Many French masters such as Jean-Léon Gérôme and Alexandre Cabanal conducted classes in their private ateliers. Another alternative was the private art school which proliferated throughout the 1870s and 1880s to absorb the overflow of students who were denied a place at the École des Beaux-Arts due to capacity enrollments or because they

FIGURE 5. *Landscape*, c. 1881, graphite on paper, 10 ¼" x 13 ¾". Collection of Mr. and Mrs. Holmes S. Adams and Mr. and Mrs. Harry M. Walker, Jackson, Mississippi.

could not pass the entrance exams. One such school was the Académie Julian, founded in 1868 to prepare students for the *concours des places* or entrance test at the Beaux-Arts.[29] Indeed it shared with the older institution a roster of famous faculty members including Gustave-Rodolphe Boulanger, Jules-Joseph Lefebvre, Adolphe-William Bouguereau and Tony Robert-Fleury. Donoho, in the company of Americans Willard Metcalf, John Twachtman, Frank Benson and Edmund Tarbell elected to study at the Académie Julian in 1880. Kenyon Cox was there as early as 1878. They were joined in 1886 by Childe Hassam whose decision to attend the school was influenced by his viewing of Donoho's painting *La Marcellerie* in 1883 when it was sent back to New York for exhibition.[30] The records of the Académie Julian were destroyed during World War II,[31] but Salon notes from 1883-1887 list Donoho as the pupil of Boulanger, Bouguereau and Lefebvre.[32]

The methods of the Académie Julian were very similar to those of the Beaux-Arts. The mastery of good draughtsmanship was a core aspect of the curriculum. Pupils were required to pass through several levels of drawing courses, beginning with the copying of engravings and plaster casts, until finally they were permitted to work from a live model. As one student described, "Construction is the main thing insisted upon at this school. No matter how good a study may be in color, if the drawing is bad, it is cut to pieces."[33] In the painting classes however, a more liberal approach to formal

FIGURE 6. *North West Knoll,* c. 1881, graphite on paper, 9 ¾" x 13 ½". Collection of Mississippi Museum of Art, Jackson. Gift of Alexander L. and Helena S. Nyerges. 1989.001.

composition was promoted. Lefebvre, Boulanger and Carolus-Duran (Charles-Emile-Auguste Durand) encouraged their painters to work quickly and to render their subjects in broad, brushy masses without an inhibiting concern for detail. Critical commentary on student work-in-progress twice a week by teams of academics from the Académie Julian and the Beaux-Arts, and weekly and monthly competitions gave added stimulus to the artist's efforts. A first place in the weekly competition meant a choice position in the ateliers for the week and a chance to enter the monthly drawing exhibition, where success meant inclusion in a painting competition with a cash prize. Students benefited from the additional instruction of the competitions and because professional exhibition experience was needed to gain recognition at the Salon.

However, as Barbara Weinberg states, the Académie Julian, unlike the Beaux-Arts, was "in effect, a trade school" which "offered only technical instruction, with no anatomy, perspective, art history, or aesthetics."[34] Moreover, its program, geared to the assimilation of standardized techniques, was criticized as turning out painters who worked in a formulaic style. As one critic remarked, "Three or four years of the Atelier Julian leaves on an artist a mark which is too easily observed...a little Julian goes a long way."[35] The environment at the Académie Julian must have suited Donoho, however, since he remained in its ateliers for seven years. Nor does his work of the 1880s suffer from a rigid

FIGURE 7. *Forge*, 1881, graphite on paper, 13 ½" x 10 ¼". Collection of Mississippi Museum of Art, Jackson. Gift of Gallery Guild. 1979.002.

adherence to the techniques of the Académie Julian, an advantage appreciated by a Boston critic when three landscape paintings were sent back to the United States for exhibition at the Pennsylvania Academy of the Fine Arts in 1882. Summarizing Donoho's progress in France, the reviewer remarked,

> *...these works are...of high order, carefully studied, yet broad in treatment, and exhibiting great reverence for*

FIGURE 8. Donoho and friend at Grez-sur-Loing, c. 1881, photograph. Gaines Ruger Donoho Papers, Archives of American Art, Smithsonian Institution, Washington, D.C. Gift of John R. Hopkins. The photograph may be a witty play on Donoho's characteristic way of ordering compositions at this time: he stands in a rowboat with his companion in a foreground dense with bracken and grass holding a long boat pole on the diagonal.

nature, coupled with a freedom of mind which saves the artist from degenerating into a slavish imitatro. The great good element in these works is the feeling of freshness that pervades them, or, in other words, the successful rendering of atmospheric effects. But beyond this must be noted the fact that the effect in each of the three landscapes is... different, showing that the artist has an open eye for nature, and has managed, so far, to keep out of a rut.[36]

FIGURE 9. Award certificate from the Cotton Centennial Exposition, New Orleans, 1885. Gaines Ruger Donoho Papers, Archives of American Art, Smithsonian Institution, Washington, D.C. Gift of John R. Hopkins.

Donoho's "open eye for nature" and keen vision of and feeling for the natural world were enhanced by his explorations of the area around Barbizon, a rural country noted for verdant woods and picturesque villages formed by rustic stone structures appropriate to a land where planted fields existed alongside wild pastures. Drawings and paintings from the early 1880s place Donoho at Grez-sur-Loing, a small village close to the forest of Fontainebleau, where a community of American artists had evolved in the previous decade. (Figures 5, 6 and 7) Judging from the limited number of photographs and memorabilia found among his personal possessions, Donoho does not seem to have been excessively sentimental. One preserved photograph in which he stands in a boat on a river near the little town attests to his attachment to this part of France. (Figure 8)

At Grez, Donoho made drawings and oil sketches of the surrounding countryside which became the basis for his first major compositions—*The Edge of the Forest* (1881), chosen for the Paris Salon that year and for the International Cotton Exposition in New Orleans in 1885, *La Marcellerie* (c. 1882), *Bad Pasture* (1882) and *Shepherd* (1884). (Figure 9) These works are filtered through the realist aesthetic and *plein-air* approach of Jules Bastien-Lepage, a painter much admired in the circles Donoho frequented[37] and known for his representations of a simple and honest, provincial people attuned to the natural world from which they gain sustenance. Donoho's vision of the Barbizon landscape reveals quiet woodlands and overgrown fields populated by French peasants. In the

FIGURE 10. *Peasants at Supper,* c. 1881-1882, graphite and charcoal on paper. Gaines Ruger Donoho Papers, Archives of American Art, Smithsonian Institution, Washington, D.C. Gift of John R. Hopkins.

paintings of this era, it is nature which absorbs the artist's attention. Human subjects are generally reduced to another aspect of the landscape. However, contemporaneous drawings document Donoho's interest in the activities of his Barbizon hosts such as in sketches made of a group of peasants at supper or the interior of a kitchen. (Figures 10 and 11)

In the great landscapes of the 1880s, his palette is subdued, dominated by related hues of muted green, grey and brown so that the surfaces are closely knit and the overall color is neither excessively warm nor cool. Donoho's use of tonal modulations for atmospheric effects and the virtual elimination of the horizon line achieves immediacy and freshness. The paintings force a recognition of the act of painting itself by way of the broadly brushed forms. Indeed, as in *La Marcellerie,* Donoho's tendency to render certain landscape elements, particularly the high grass and tree line, as abstract linear strokes, was criticized on the grounds that it led to a work "sum-

marily treated for a picture that purports to be finished."[38] (Figure 12) It is this surprisingly modern sense of the autonomous functions of the pictorial components which distinguishes his work from that of Bastien-Lepage's.[39] The French artist's works manifest a devotion to mimetic detail while Donoho transcribes his subjects more loosely and expressively, allowing color and line to operate with some degree of autonomy in the interest of pictorial unity. In *Shepherd* the vertical composition features a man dressed in a lambswool coat and brown felt cap whose weather-beaten face bears an expression suggesting he has been startled into alertness by something or someone not revealed to the viewer. (PLATE 1) The intensely active brushwork of the rough wind-tossed grasses, unkempt thistledown bushes and fresh green pastures beyond dominate the work rather than the human subject. One reviewer enthusiastically responded to the *Shepherd* as seeming so real in conception that he imagined the peasant "shouting excitedly to his dog to gather in the sheep, which are seen in the distance roaming off at their own sweet will."[40] Yet the "reality" of the painting

FIGURE 11. *Interior of a Kitchen*, signed "Lavoir, Barbizon, France, Ruger Donoho, 1890," pencil and charcoal on paper. Gaines Ruger Donoho Papers, Archives of American Art, Smithsonian Institution, Washington, D.C. Gift of John R. Hopkins.

FIGURE 12. *La Marcellerie,* c. 1882, oil on canvas, 51 3/8" x 77 1/8". Collection of The Brooklyn Museum, New York. Gift of George A. Hearn. 11.533.

is more directly transmitted by the coarse, highly tactile strokes with which Donoho orchestrates the natural scenery.

Both *La Marcellerie* and *Bad Pasture* were selected for the Salon exhibitions of 1882 and 1883, respectively, and the former would earn Donoho a silver medal at the Paris Universal Exposition of 1889. *La Marcellerie,* along with the painting *Explorers* (c. 1883), also garnered an honorable mention at the Columbian Exposition in Chicago in 1893. Donoho must have found it extremely gratifying that Shirlaw, one of his teachers at the Art Students League, was on the judges' panel for the Columbian Exposition.[41] (Figure 13) Apart from one negative review by a critic who rather sourly complained that *La Marcellerie* was "painfully monotonous in color and scattered in effect,"[42] it was uniformly praised by American artists and critics. Whistler commended the work as "the very finest landscape" and Hassam, who viewed the work when it was shown at the National Academy of Design in 1883, pronounced it "the best out-of-door picture painted by an American painter at that time...."[43] The critic Charles Kurtz deemed it "an unusually excellent landscape study" and reproduced the composition as a line drawing in his *Illustrated Art Notes,* published on the occasion of the National Academy of Design's annual show of 1883.[44] Kenyon Cox, respected by his compatriots for both his artistic skills and critical judgement and Donoho's fellow student at the Académie

Julian, maintained "Mr. Donoho is a painter who has produced too little and exhibited too little of what he has produced, but this picture [*La Marcellerie*], decoratively designed and closely studied shows us a talent at once robust and fine."[45]

American critic Roger Riordan described *Bad Pasture* as "composed of a foreground of tangled weeds and saplings... through which a peasant and two shaggy calves are forcing their way," and *Primroses* (c. 1882) as a "picture of a Normandy woman in a light blue gown... picking primroses in a grassy valley at the foot of a hill which mounts almost to the top of the canvas."[46] When the paintings were shown at the Pennsylvania Academy of the Fine Arts in 1883 both elicited a positive reaction. Riordan noted "The coloring is cool but natural and harmonious, and the drawing and relief and the rendering of the qualities of the atmosphere is excellent." The American artist Sanford Gifford's homage to the work of Donoho's French Barbizon predecessors Jean-Baptiste-Camille Corot and Charles-François Daubigny could apply equally as well to the American:

> *In the French landscape everything like finish and elaboration of detail is sacrificed to the unity of the effect to be produced. Every "prettiness" of execution is ignored utterly. Nothing is allowed to interfere with that unity.... The subjects are mostly of the simplest and most meager description; but by the remarkable truth of color and tone, joined to a poetic perception of the beauty of common things, they are made beautiful.*[47]

UNITED STATES
Department K.—Fine Arts.
Exhibitor G. Ruger Donoho, Address New Y k.
Group 140. Class
Exhibit Oil Paintings.
AWARD
La Marcelleris.
Explorers.
Signed Walter Shirlaw,
Individual Judge
Approved H. W. B. Davis,
Approved
Chairman Executive Committee on Awards
Copyist R. P. C. Date Mar. 9, 1894.

FIGURE 13. Award certificate from Painting Exhibition, Columbian Exposition, Chicago, 1894. Gaines Ruger Donoho Papers, Archives of American Art, Smithsonian Institution, Washington, D.C. Gift of John R. Hopkins. The document is signed by Walter Shirlaw, Donoho's former teacher and one of the judges at the Columbian Exposition.

Concepts articulated by Gifford in his description of Barbizon painting, such as "the unity of the effect to be produced" and "the remarkable truth of color and tone," are also characteristic of the Impressionist agenda which Donoho partially adopted at the turn of the century. French Impressionists were showing their works throughout the 1880s and Impressionist ideas were beginning to seep into academic theory. However, American artists working in Paris during the early and mid-part of the decade were not, on the whole, attracted to the

FIGURE 14. View of Town Pond at East Hampton, c. 1900, photograph. Gaines Ruger Donoho Papers, Archives of American Art, Smithsonian Institution, Washington, D.C. Gift of John R. Hopkins.

new style. The conservatism among American artists trained in Europe, even American Impressionists, reflected a sustained devotion to the fundamentals of academic picture-making.[48] Donoho seems to have eschewed the kind of stylistic transformations being wrought by the French Impressionist group, preferring to emulate the example set by early adherents of *plein-airism* such as Corot and Pierre Étienne-Théodore Rousseau. Yet, almost in spite of his more conservative attitude, Donoho achieves a balance between the traditional compositional order taught at the Académie Julian and the growing awareness of the significance of elements such as color and line apart from their figurative or mimetic functions through his insistence upon the tangible painterly mark.

A self-portrait selected for the Paris Salon in 1886 suggests Donoho's familiarity with a kind of Symbolist appreciation for the artistic evocation of an expressive mood, as in the works of Whistler and Puvis de Chavannes. (PLATE 2) Portraits are rare among Donoho's oeuvre. Perhaps the artist chose this genre specifically as a means of investigating the power of color and brushstroke to probe that most intangible of subjects, the human psyche. He appears in a three-quarter, centralized pose, his introspective gaze directed just above that of the viewer. The very embodiment of the stereotypical nineteenth-century artist, he is dressed in a voluminous green coat with a great tan cravat and beret, an ensemble fittingly embellished by the beard and large mustache obscuring his mouth. His long face with its high cheekbones, shadowed eyes and wide expanse of illuminated forehead—a time-honored physiognomic metaphor for the light of intellect—bespeaks a sensitive personality while the red of his hair marks him as being of creative temperament. Undoubtedly, Donoho resembled the individual represented in the portrait but the generally muted palette and fluid brushwork suggest that he was seeking to communicate more than a veristic report of his physical appearance. The surface of the portrait, in contrast to his earlier landscapes, is painted very thinly with pale grey-green hues. In the background, against this misty region of color, is a screen of leafless attenuated trees, more decorative than descriptive in effect. The vertical orientation of the work and a high horizon line cause a flattening of space in which there is little recession into depth. A fusion of the pictorial planes, the pervasiveness of the green atmosphere, a melding of the brushstrokes describing the sleeve of his coat and the shadowy patches of grass behind him and the absence of hard-edged contour lines make it seem as though the figure of the artist has emerged out of the dreamy landscape. The result is a powerfully symbolic image. As in the works of Puvis de Chavannes, the external world of nature becomes a conduit to the realm of Donoho's imagination.

Returning to New York in 1887, having distinguished himself in France as one of the most promising artists of his generation, Donoho set up a professional studio at 146 West 55th Street, not far from the Art Students League.[49] It is likely that he was offered a membership at the National Academy of Design but if so, Donoho must have declined. Instead he joined the Society of American Artists. His decision may have been made for political reasons because the Society of American Artists was a breakaway organization of artists disenchanted with the protectionist, isolationist stance maintained by the conservative board of the National Academy. In 1888, Donoho's *Self-Portrait* (1886) and *Night* (c. 1887-1888) hung in the annual show of the Society of American Artists. The Society awarded him the Webb prize in 1892.[50] In 1889 Donoho won the silver medal at the Paris Universal Exposition for *La Marcellerie.* Among his American co-exhibitors (most of them his friends) including Chase, Beckwith, Hassam and J. Alden Weir, only the venerable Whistler, who received the Legion of Honor, earned a higher award at the Exposition.

Once back in New York, Donoho seems to have devoted himself to his career. He regularly sent works for exhibition in this country and abroad and joined artists' associations such as the Players Club, an informal art group where younger artists, many of them Paris-trained, met to discuss their work.[51] At this juncture, having made a name for himself in the two venues most critical to an artist's success, Donoho's star was on the ascent. Inexplicably, in 1890 he curtailed his day-to-day involvement with the art world and later in that year left New York for Long Island settling in

FIGURE 15. Bridal portrait of Matilda Ackley Donoho, 1894, photograph. Gaines Ruger Donoho Papers, Archives of American Art, Smithsonian Institution, Washington, D.C. Gift of John R. Hopkins.

what was then the remote township of East Hampton.

At the time of Donoho's precipitous move, the eastern end of Long Island did not have the glamorous cachet it acquired in the next century. It was a bucolic region of planted fields, sandy beaches and grassy meadows punctuated by small villages untouched by the physical encroachments of industrial civilization and characterized by a slow, rustic way of life. East Hampton was a farm community specializing in chickens and dairy cows. As a town its most notable features were century-old shingled cottages, an old graveyard, a public pond and two working windmills. (Figure 14) Lacking sophistication and many of the modern amenities to which the city-dweller was accustomed, it offered a respite for the urban vacationer anxious to escape the stresses and fast-pace of city life but it was not a place in which high culture flourished easily. And yet, beginning in the mid-1870s, East Hampton exercised a peculiar fascination for American artists, particularly those who, like Donoho, had spent a significant amount of time in Europe.

Members of the Tile Club, an informal group of artists and writers based in New York, communicated to their associates in the city the geographical and spiritual attractions of the Long Island "wilderness." On a foray to the Hamptons in 1878, the Tilers were overwhelmed by the unspoiled beauty of the landscape and the simple existence of the native population and promoted their discovery as the New World equivalent of pastoral sites such as Brittany and Barbizon.[52] Based on the accounts of the Tile Club *Scribners Monthly*

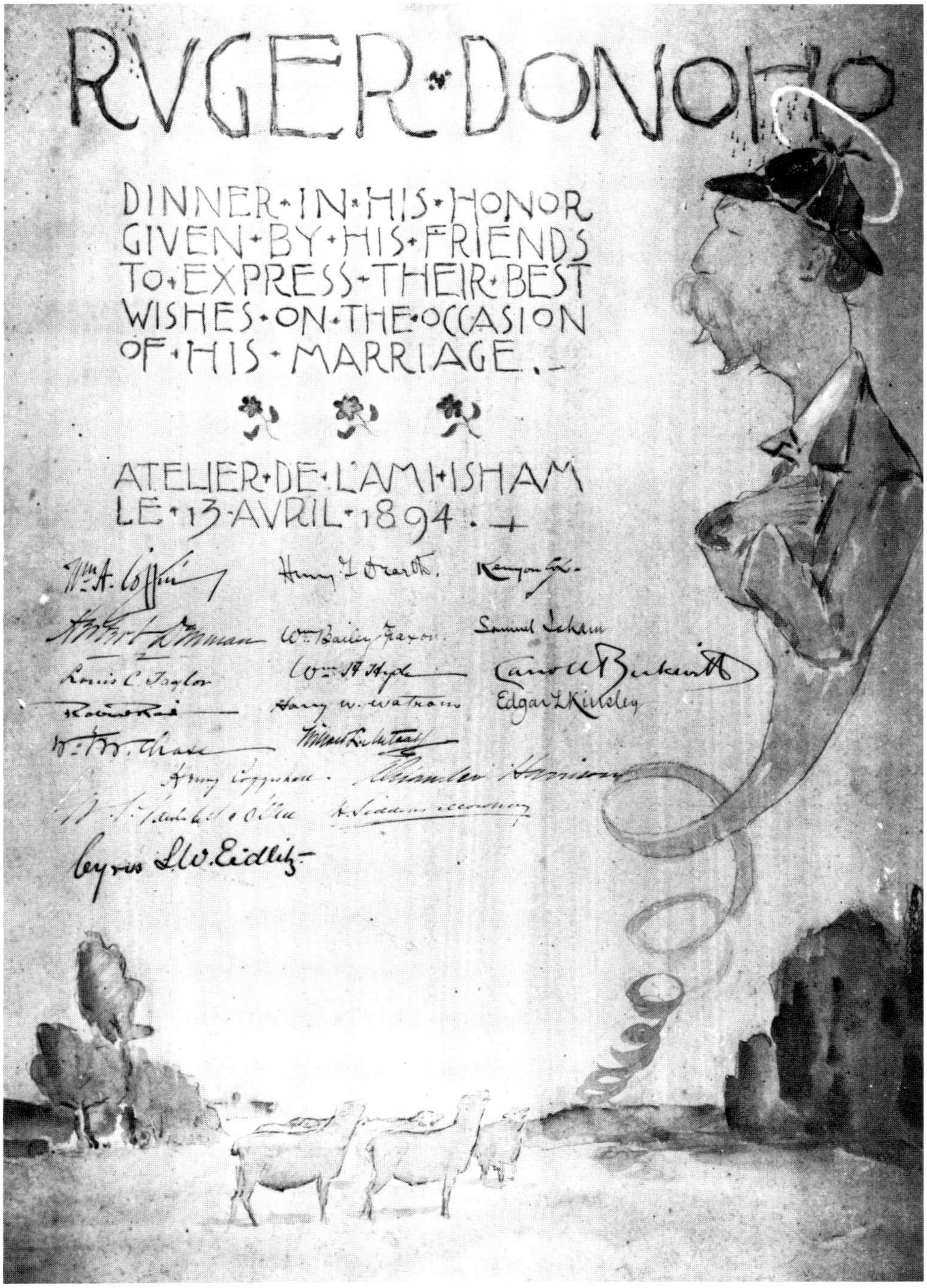

FIGURE 16.
Illustrated menu for banquet celebrating the Donoho nuptials, dated "13 Avril 1894," watercolor and ink on paper. Gaines Ruger Donoho Papers, Archives of American Art, Smithsonian Institution, Washington, D.C. Gift of John R. Hopkins. Signatures include Kenyon Cox, William Merritt Chase, John Carroll Beckwith, Willard Metcalf, Robert Reid, Alexander Harrison and William Coffin.

Magazine, a popular journal of the era, noted the interest the area held for artists remarking that they were "carried away...by the hay ricks, the poultry yards, the winding sheep, the returning herds lost in a maze of soft grey atmosphere so like their beloved Barbizon."[53] Writing for *Lippincott's Magazine* in 1882, the journalist Charles Burr Todd christened East Hampton "the American Barbizon."[54]

By the early 1880s a small and close-knit artists' colony was thriving on these far-flung shores of the Atlantic. Thomas Moran, already famous for his depictions of the American West, established year-round residence in East Hampton in 1882. His home, nicknamed "The Studio," served as a hub for visiting artists such as Shirlaw, Gifford and Donoho. Chase founded the Shinnecock Art School in neighboring Southampton in 1891 and though Donoho was not affiliated with the program, Chase was a close friend.

Donoho decided to make his home in East Hampton in 1891, buying an extensive piece of property at the foot of Egypt Lane near the end of the village. Judging from the expanse of his land and the substantial house he built there in 1894, Donoho must have enjoyed considerable financial prosperity. A description of the house appeared in the East Hampton newspaper *The Star* in January 1895 when Donoho became the first town resident with a new-fangled "Furman hot water heater."

> *Mr. Ruger Donoho, on Egypt Lane, is now prepared to enjoy the winter weather.... A Furman hot water heater has recently been installed in his house... and begun its beneficent mission of warming to a temperature of 70 or more degrees, on Saturday last. Ten rooms are heated, including a large studio.*[55]

The thirty-seven year old Donoho's commitment to domesticity coincided with his marriage on April 13, 1894, to Matilda Ackley of Philadelphia. Her bridal portrait, discovered among Donoho's papers, depicts a slender dark-haired young woman of quiet, self-possessed beauty. (Figure 15) After her death in 1939, an East Hampton friend recalled, "Unobtrusive, shy, and hating prominence in any gathering, Mrs. Donoho could not yet hide from us her fine, strong character, her salty wisdom."[56] From this description, one suspects that she and her talented, modest husband were ideally suited in temperament.

The Donoho nuptials took place in New York in a decidely artistic milieu—the studio of Samuel Isham. Beckwith recorded in his diary, "We gave Donoho a bachelors dinner, he is to be married next week, up in Johanni's studio. It was very jolly...."[57] The esteem in which Donoho was held by his artist friends is reflected in the illustrated menu they conceived for his wedding banquet. On it a charming ink and watercolor drawing represents the apotheosis of the painter, complete with halo and an adoring flock of sheep, as he hovers above a bucolic landscape which looks suspiciously like Barbizon but could also be Long Island. The memento is signed by several New York art world luminaries including William Coffin, William Merritt Chase, Alexander Harrison, J. Carroll Beckwith, Willard Metcalf, Robert Reid and Kenyon Cox. (Figure 16)

Although Donoho continued to maintain his own studio in New York,[58] the couple regarded East Hampton as their primary residence. Unlike most of the artists in his circle who spent only the summer months on Long Island, the Donohos became entrenched in the community. They befriended natives such as Jonathan Fithian, a dairy farmer whose pastures, just across the way from the Donoho house, were depicted in many canvases. In an account of the lands adjacent to the Donoho property, one of his local acquaintances remarked upon Donoho's passion for the Fithian farm:

...we rested our eyes on the deep green bracken, and the elderberry and the blackberry, just coming into white bloom. It is even more beautiful in spring, when the shadbush and beach-plum are out, or in autumn, when it is purple with wild asters and gold, russet, and brown with the changing leaves...

FIGURE 17. Drawing for Presidential banner in support of Theodore Roosevelt, 1892, watercolor, ink and graphite on paper, 11" x 7 ⅞". Collection of East Hampton Library, Long Island Collection, New York.

FIGURE 18. *Woodhouse Water Garden*, 1911, oil on canvas, 24" x 34". Collection of Guild Hall Museum, East Hampton, New York. Gift of Mrs. Lorenzo E. Woodhouse, 1931. 31.3.

in the early winter, when the first riot of color has passed, and the tones are a little subdued, the whole meadow takes on the colors of a fine old Persian rug.... When Mr. Donoho first came to East Hampton in 1890, and began to paint our beauty spots and quiet lanes, that was one of the places he loved best.[59]

Despite the withdrawn, introspective image presented in his self-portrait of 1886, Donoho seems to have been quite a sociable sort of man. He joined the Maidstone Club, an exclusive country club, and helped lobby for its golf course.[60] For the 1892 presidential election, he organized a torchlight parade through the streets of East Hampton in support of Teddy Roosevelt. Donoho marched at the head of the parade with fellow-artist Emil Carlsen with whom he carried a sixteen-foot-long banner bearing a portrait drawing of the candidate and the slogan "The People's Choice."[61] (Figure 17) Matilda Donoho was instrumental in establishing the East Hampton Garden Club and devoted considerable effort to the protection of the natural areas and indigenous wildlife. In 1934, in memory of her husband, she deeded eight acres of the former Fithian pastures to the village as part of the Woodhouse Gardens, an adjacent nature conservancy.[62] She also served as something of a town historian, researching and writing historical essays for the local newspaper.[63]

Donoho's enjoyment of his small-town citizenship did not, however, distract him from pursuing his professional calling. Indeed he seemed to revel in the artistic possibilities inherent in his surroundings. If he had moved to East Hampton in the hopes of finding the same kind of inspiration which resulted in his best Barbizon paintings, his brush quickly adapted to the unique beauty of his American setting. Donoho's paintings of the early 1890s feature the generic pastoral subjects familiar from his successful Barbizon landscapes—sheep, weathered farmhouses and outbuildings, wooded copses and yards of green foliage growing up and across a rich brown earthen ground. Works such as *East Hampton Garden, Late Afternoon Winter* and *Study of Sheep in Woods, East Hampton* conform to the diagonal composition characteristic of his Salon works. (PLATES 3, 14 and 4) Yet the later American pictures show a light palette and forego subtle tonal harmonies in favor of saturated hues capable of simulating bright, strong sunlight. These changes are especially evident in *Late Afternoon Winter*, a snow scene in which the roof of cottages and a dirt path suddenly glow pure white when caught in the light of a morning sun crossing through the icy blue of the surrounding fields. In *Study of Sheep in Woods, East Hampton,* a dazzling light turns the livestock into a mass of white fleece and arrays the deep green foliage in a dappled pattern of light and shadow made tactile through Donoho's impasto touch.

The early East Hampton works herald Donoho's transition to a personal variant of the Impressionist style. His willingness to experiment with a style he had previously shunned may have been due to his rekindled friendship with Childe Hassam who rented Donoho's carriage house beginning in 1898.[64] The short, broken, densely-woven brushstrokes and highly-keyed color contrasts characteristic of Hassam's paintings are evident in many of Donoho's canvases. But curiously, Donoho's Impressionist works exhibit a crisp delineation of form that is not found in his earlier works. Moreover, he seems to have reserved an Impressionist style for one particular subject—his own flower gardens and those of the neighboring Woodhouse Gardens. Impressionism, with its emphasis on color and light, may have been the most appropriate style for capturing scenes with which he was so passionately involved that, as one reviewer wrote he "could not let any part of the feast of color go."[65] As the critic Royal Cortissoz noted, "He painted that garden over and over again in the same spirit in which he pottered over its flowers and hedges, loving it all and understanding it."[66]

Cortissoz's comment implies a comparison of Donoho with the French painter Claude Monet, ensconced in his own garden paradise at Giverny. By the 1890s, Monet's Impressionism had evolved into nearly abstract veils of shimmering paint different in conception from Donoho's American realist version but similarly inspired by the beauty of a Japanese water garden landscape. Directly across from the Donoho estate, the Woodhouse Gardens were renowned for a Japanese water garden fashioned from a swamp in 1901 by Mrs. Lorenzo G. Woodhouse. Flanked at the entrance by two tea houses and covering almost three acres, it included two lily ponds traversed by bright red Japanese bridges. The flower beds were planted with purple and white irises punctuated with pale pink and red blossoms.[67] This was the site recorded in Donoho's monumental *Woodhouse Water Garden* (1911), a vibrant composition in which lily pads float between the reflections of trees upon a green pond banked by a meandering fence and hundreds of blossoms arranged in striations of brilliant color. (Figure 18) The same dazzling coloristic effects are achieved in *Wind Flowers* (1912), where the colored air itself seems permeated by the scent of the blossoms stirred by the breeze. (PLATE 15) In *A Garden* (1911) the upper story of a house in the background is barely visible amid the riotous display of flowers and foliage blanketing the fore- and middle-grounds. (PLATE 12) *A Garden* was awarded an honorable mention at the Carnegie Institute's Annual Exhibition of 1911[68] and a gold medal at the Panama-Pacific International Exposition held in San Francisco in 1915. It was also shown in New York at the Armory Show of 1913. The painter J. Alden Weir, in his capacity of curator for The Metropolitan Museum of Art, selected *Wind Flowers* for the collection just after the artist's death in 1916.

Even as Donoho celebrated the gardens of East Hampton as joyous fields of color and light, he was simultaneously engaged in painting a lesser-known side of the region. From 1890 onward, Donoho presented the fields and beaches of

Long Island as dark nocturnal regions of shifting form and shadow. Modulated hues of deep greens and blues create dark chromatic fields punctuated at intervals by flecks of glimmering light and turn Donoho's night landscapes into powerful tonal poems. In *Trees of Heaven No. 2* (c. 1890), *Egypt Beach in the Moonlight* (c. 1898-1899) and *Home Sweet Home* (c. 1899) the familiar world of the village vanishes, replaced by a dream place in which ghostly figures parade solemnly down a dark shoreline and dimly lit forbidding structures offer entrance. Arboreal groupings loom large, casting fantastic shadows upon the ground. In a sense these late nocturnes achieved the kind of formal, metaphoric unities Donoho sought to discover twenty years earlier in France. (PLATES 5 and 7)

Donoho died at the age of fifty-nine in the spring of 1916. A memorial exhibition at the Macbeth Gallery in New York was organized by his friends under the direction of Childe Hassam who wrote movingly of Donoho in the catalogue, "An artist is a person who pursues his calling in quiet and solitude and is only known by his own kind. Ruger Donoho had a great deal of this kind of recognition, and if he did not have as much of the world's recognition as many others, or as much as he deserved, all is well."[69] After viewing the exhibition which included works from 1884 until the year of the artist's death, Thomas Dewing wrote in a letter to Matilda Donoho: "I can only say that Ruger was a great painter. I see this more clearly than ever before...I shall say to everybody as I always have, how great they are and what a great impression they make when seen together."[70] It could not have escaped Dewing that Donoho's works "when seen together," successfully embodied the forces which shaped late nineteenth-century American art.

Notes

1. Childe Hassam, *Memorial Exhibition: Paintings by the Late Ruger Donoho* (exhibition catalogue) (New York: Macbeth Gallery, 1916), n.p. Hassam later recalled that Whistler and Puvis were particularly impressed by Donoho's *La Marcellerie* (c. 1882), praising it as "the very finest landscape." Hassam, "Interview" (1927), De Witt McClellan Lockman Papers, Archives of American Art, Smithsonian Institution: Roll 503.

2. Hassam, *Memorial Exhibition*, n.p.

3. Church Hill, Jefferson County, record #700. Department of Archives and History, Jackson, Mississippi.

4. Church Hill was settled by families from Virginia and Maryland. According to a census

taken in 1830, several Donoho families were living in the area around Church Hill, Mississippi, at this time. Two territorial petitions bear the signature of Gaines Donoho. Department of Archives and History, Jackson, Mississippi.

5. Church Hill is located in the western part of Jefferson County and can be found by following a dirt road west from U.S. Highway 61 for approximately two miles. Church Hill, Jefferson County, record #700.

6. Ibid.

7. Gaines Ruger Donoho as quoted by Hassam in *Memorial Exhibition*, n.p.

8. Ibid.

9. Thomas Howard Ruger achieved the rank of general during the Civil War and was decorated by the government for his heroic contributions to the Union cause. See Ezra J. Warner, *Generals in Blue, Lives of the Union Commanders* (Baton Rouge, Louisiana: Louisiana State University Press, 1964), pp. 415-16.

10. Hassam, *Memorial Exhibition*, n.p.

11. *Boyd's Directory of the District of Columbia, Together with a Compendium of Its Governments, Institutions, and Trades* (Washington, D.C., 1874), n.p. In subsequent editions of the same directory her addresses are given as 1323 H Street, N.W., in 1877 and 1007 G Street in 1882.

12. James H. Whyte, *The Uncivil War: Washington During the Reconstruction, 1865-1878* (New York: Twayne Publishers, 1958), p. 95. Whyte notes, "Buck and Jesse [Grant] attended the Emerson Institute on 14th Street, where they were driven each morning by an orderly in a cart drawn by a pair of Shetland ponies."

13. "Emerson Past and Present" (catalogue) (Washington, D.C.: Emerson Institute, 1926), n.p. The school was founded in 1852 and remains in operation today.

14. *Boyd's Directory of the District of Columbia* (Washington, D.C., 1877), p. 243.

15. Julia Donoho. Letter to Jervis McEntee, 1878, Feinberg Papers, Archives of American Art, Smithsonian Institution: Roll D30.

16. Organized in 1825 along the lines of the model offered by its older European counterparts, the primary mission of the National Academy was to educate and train young artists. To that end, an Antique School where students were instructed in the rudiments of classical design principles was founded in 1827. In the traditional academic manner, they learned how to render the human figure in space by copying plaster casts of antique and Renaissance sculptures. Additional materials for practice in drawing were offered through the Academy's library which contained folios of engravings of European masterworks and exercise copybooks. More advanced students were allowed to progress to the Life School, opened in 1837, where they could paint and draw directly from nude models. A lecture series featuring prominent artists as well as men-of-letters was introduced in 1826. The Academy also sponsored an annual exhibition devoted to the works of contemporary artists in a novel departure from the policies of other arts academies where annual shows were, by and large, dominated by the already validated works of dead masters. Thus the National Academy of Design, though it was never able to achieve the artistic hegemony of its counterparts abroad,

fulfilled an important need in American art education and helped to spur the development of what was still a nascent field in this country. See Lois Marie Fink and Joshua C. Taylor, *Academy: The Academic Tradition in American Art* (Chicago and London: The University of Chicago Press, 1978), pp. 5-6. For a more detailed analysis of the curriculum of the National Academy of Design see the earlier comprehensive version of this text, *Academy: The Academic Tradition in American Art, An Exhibition Organized on the Occasion of the One Hundred and Fiftieth Anniversary of the National Academy of Design: 1825-1975* (Washington, D.C.: Smithsonian Institution Press, 1975), pp. 29-37.

17. Registration card dated 1878-1879 for Gaines Ruger Donoho, Record Office of the Art Students League, New York.

18. Disagreements among the governing board concerning the funding of the school's operation came to a head in the 1870s when it was proposed by a faction within the administration with the support of President Thomas Worthington Wittredge that the life classes be discontinued as an insupportable expense. It was further recommended that Professor Lemuel Wilmarth, hired in 1870 to serve as Director of the Schools, be discharged. Fink and Taylor, *Academy: The Academic Tradition in American Art*, 1975, pp. 51-58.

19. Marchel E. Langren, *Years of Art: The Story of the Art Students League of New York* (New York: Art Students League, 1940), pp. 21-27. See also Frank Walker, *First Report of the Art Students League of New York* (New York: Art Students League, 1886).

20. Fink and Taylor, *Academy: The Academic Tradition in American Art*, 1975, p. 55.

21. "Art Students League, Prospectus, 1875," as quoted in Langren, *Years of Art*, p. 18.

22. *Paris Salon: Explication des Oeuvrages de Peinture* (Paris: 1881 and 1882), n.p.

23. Ronald Pisano, *G. Ruger Donoho (1857-1916), A Retrospective Exhibition* (exhibition catalogue) (New York: Hirschl & Adler Galleries, 1977), no. 6, n.p.

24. Fink and Taylor, *Academy: The Academic Tradition in American Art*, 1975, pp. 59-60.

25. George W. Sheldon, *American Painters* (New York, 1978), p. 51.

26. Architectural detailing was apparently a passion with Donoho. Hassam related that the house he rented from his friend in East Hampton in the 1890s had "hand hammered hinges, and if one was gone, Mr. Donoho would say take this down to the village blacksmith and get another." Hassam, "Interview" (1927).

27. Lois Marie Fink, *American Art at the Nineteenth-Century Paris Salons* (Cambridge: Cambridge University Press, 1990), p. 283.

28. The École des Beaux-Arts, in addition to boasting the most accomplished art faculty of all the schools in France, was tuition-free to students of all nationalities.

29. H. Barbara Weinberg, *The Lure of Paris: Nineteenth-Century American Painters and Their French Teachers* (New York: Abbeville Press, 1991), p. 221.

30. Hassam, "Interview" (1927).

31. Weinberg, p. 222.

32. Donoho is listed in the Salon records as the

pupil of R. Swain Gifford for the years 1881 and 1882. In 1883 and 1884 Boulanger and Lefebvre are credited as his teachers. The latter is also cited in 1885, 1886 and 1887 along with Bouguereau. *Paris Salon: Explication des Oeuvrages de Peinture* (Paris: 1881-1887), n.p.

33. Daisy Brown, "Experiences at the Julian School," *Corcoran Art Journal* 1 (April 1893), p. 6.

34. Weinberg, p. 226.

35. Ibid., p. 223.

36. "Art in Philadelphia. The Galleries of the Pennsylvania Academy," *Boston Daily Advertiser*, November 18, 1882, Archives of American Art, Smithsonian Institution: Roll 53.

37. The work of Jules Bastien-Lepage was admired by many Paris-trained American artists of Donoho's generation. See Weinberg, pp.123-24, 243.

38. *Boston Daily Advertiser.*

39. See Julia R. Meyers, "The American Expatriate Painters of the French Peasantry, 1863-1893," Ph.D dissertation. University of Maryland, 1989, p. 261.

40. "The Paris Salon," *Art Amateur* 11 no. 1 (June 1884), p. 5.

41. Notice of Award to G. Ruger Donoho, signed Walter Shirlaw, Individual Judge, Feinberg Papers, Archives of American Art, Smithsonian Institution: Roll 3667.

42. "Fine Arts. The Sixth Annual Exhibition of the Society of American Artists," *The Nation* 12 no. 928 (April 12, 1883), p. 328.

43. Hassam, "Interview" (1927).

44. The line drawing of *La Marcellerie* was executed by James D. Smillie. Charles M. Kurtz, ed. *Illustrated Art Notes upon the Fifty-Eighth Annual Exhibition of the National Academy of Design, New York* (New York: National Academy of Design, 1883), p. 47.

45. Kenyon Cox, as quoted in Helen Earle, *Biographical Sketches of American Artists* (Michigan, 1924), p. 101.

46. Roger Riordan, "The Exhibition of the Pennsylvania Academy of Fine Arts," *Art Amateur* 10 no. 1 (December 1883), p. 7.

47. Sanford Gifford, as quoted in Peter Bermingham, *American Art in the Barbizon Mood* (Washington, D.C.: National Collection of Fine Arts, Smithsonian Institution Press, 1975), p. 52.

48. Weinberg, pp. 244-47.

49. This is the address given in the exhibition catalogue of the Society of American Artists in which Donoho participated in 1888. See Pisano. There is little evidence about how Donoho supported himself. He probably derived some income from the sale of his works although commissions are not recorded. It is possible that he had a small independent income. After Donoho's death in 1916, a series of letters exchanged between his wife, Matilda Ackley Donoho, and Robert Macbeth of the Macbeth Gallery concerning the sale of Donoho's works refer to her financial difficulties. See Macbeth Gallery Papers, Archives of American Art, Smithsonian Institution: Roll NMc43.

50. Donoho's friend, John Carroll Beckwith, who was on the jury for the Society of American Artists exhibition of 1892, noted in a journal entry

dated April 28, 1892: "Gave the Webb prize to Donoho and the Show purchase to Robinson. The exhibition is a very swell one indeed. . . ." John Carroll Beckwith Papers, Archives of American Art, Smithsonian Institution: Roll 4799.

51. Hassam, "Interview" (1927).

52. "The Tile Club at Play," *Scribners Monthly Magazine* (February 1879), p. 21.

53. Katharine Cameron, "East Hampton: The 19th Century Artist's Paradise," (East Hampton, New York: Guild Hall Museum, 1991), n.p.

54. Ibid.

55. *The Star*, January 20, 1895. Donoho may have refurbished an older, colonial structure. Childe Hassam later purchased from his widow a pre-revolutionary cottage on the Donoho property which he described as "one of the first houses ever built by one of the earliest English settlers there..." which Donoho "had spent much time in remodeling." Hassam, "Interview" (1927).

56. Mary Paxton Hamlin, "A Tribute to the Late Mrs. Ruger Donoho," *The Star*, August 3, 1939, p. 2.

57. John Carroll Beckwith Papers, Archives of American Art: 4799:1503.

58. Donoho maintained a studio in New York at 130 West 57th Street at least as late as 1903.

59. "One of Ours," *The Star*, June 23, 1938, vol. 53, p. 305.

60. The membership of the Maidstone Club was dominated by wealthy summer visitors. See "Summer Colony Life Centers at Maidstone Club," *The Star*, October 24, 1935, pp. 5-6.

61. *The Star*, November 1, 1892, p. 1.

62. Edna B. King, "The Nature Trail, Village of East Hampton," unpublished manuscript, East Hampton Library.

63. For example, see Matilda A. Donoho, "East Hampton in 1890, Or, Boarding House Days," *The Star*, October 24, 1935.

64. Matilda Donoho sold the cottage and some land to Hassam in 1919.

65. *The Sun*, November 19, 1916, Macbeth Gallery Papers, Archives of American Art, Smithsonian Institution: Roll NMc2.

66. Royal Cortissoz, "An Artist Made Better Known Since His Death," *Tribune* (November 1916), Macbeth Gallery Papers.

67. Enez Whipple, "The Japanese Water Garden and Nature Trail," October 15, 1984, unpublished manuscript, East Hampton Library.

68. John W. Beatty, Director of Fine Arts, Carnegie Institute. Letter to G. Ruger Donoho, August 9, 1911, Carnegie Papers, Archives of American Art, Smithsonian Institution: Record 3412.

69. Hassam, *Memorial Exhibition*, n.p.

70. Thomas Dewing. Letter to Matilda Donoho, November 14, 1917, Donoho Papers, Archives of American Art, Smithsonian Institution: Roll 3667.

PLATE 1. *Shepherd*, 1884, oil on canvas, 71 ⅜" x 47 ½". Collection of National Museum of American Art, Smithsonian Institution, Washington, D.C. Gift of John R. Hopkins. 1975.114.

PLATE 2. *Self-Portrait*, 1886, oil on canvas, 24 ¾" x 19 ⅝". Collection of Mississippi Museum of Art, Jackson. Gift of Gallery Guild. 1979.001.

PLATE 3. *East Hampton Garden*, c. 1890, oil on canvas, 14" x 24". Collection of The Museums at Stony Brook, New York. Museum Purchase, 1989. 89.14.

PLATE 4. *Study of Sheep in Woods, East Hampton*, c. 1890, oil on canvas, 25 ¼" x 30". Collection of Mississippi Museum of Art, Jackson. Gift of Dr. and Mrs. Beckett Howorth, by exchange. 1992.027.

PLATE 5. *Trees of Heaven No. 2*, c. 1890, oil on canvas, 25" x 30". Collection of James J. Shields, New York, New York.

PLATE 6. *Sheep, Late Afternoon*, 1891, oil on canvas, 24" x 44". Collection of Greenville County Museum of Art, South Carolina. Purchase, with funds from Mr. and Mrs. Christie C. Prevost. 85.21.11.

PLATE 7. *Egypt Beach in the Moonlight*, c. 1898-1899, oil on canvas, 16" x 30". Collection of Dan Flavin, Wainscott, New York.

PLATE 8. *Summer Night*, c. 1898-1899, oil on canvas, 20" x 24". Collection of James J. Shields, New York, New York.

PLATE 9.
Moonlight, Mills at Pont Aven, c. 1900, oil on canvas, 30" x 36". Collection of High Museum of Art, Atlanta, Georgia. Purchase. 31.6.

PLATE 10. *Auratum Lilies*, 1907, oil on canvas, 24" x 20". Collection of May and Frederick Hill, New York, New York.

PLATE II. *Wet Snow, Marlotte,* 1907, oil on canvas, 20" x 24". Collection of Mr. and Mrs. Charles C. Mickel, Greenville, South Carolina.

PLATE 12. *A Garden,* 1911, oil on canvas, 30" x 36". Collection of Art Gallery of Ontario, Toronto, Canada. Gift of Canadian National Exhibition Association, 1965. 97.

PLATE 13. *Blossom Time, Right of Path, Marlotte,* c. 1911, oil on canvas, 24" x 20". Collection of Mississippi Museum of Art, Jackson. Gift of Mrs. Velma Jernigan Rodgers. 1981.272.

PLATE 14. *Late Afternoon Winter,* c. 1911, oil on canvas, 30" x 36". Collection of New Orleans Museum of Art, Louisiana. Purchase, with funds from Major Benjamin Morgan Harrod Fund. 30.1.

PLATE 15. *Wind Flowers,* 1912, oil on canvas, 30" x 36". Collection of The Metropolitan Museum of Art, New York, New York. Rogers Fund, 1917. 17.36.

PLATE 16. *The Garden Steps,* c. 1913, oil on canvas, 15 ⅛" x 18 ⅛". Collection of Mississippi Museum of Art, Jackson. Gift of W.E. Walker Foundation. 1978.036.

Chronology

1857 Gaines Ruger Donoho born on December 21 to Robert and Julia Ruger Donoho at Church Hill, Mississippi. Spends his early years on his father's plantation in Jefferson County.

1860-1863 The Civil War begins in 1860. Robert Donoho, the artist's father, dies in 1862.

1864 Donoho and his mother, Julia Ruger Donoho, flee Church Hill with the assistance of a division of Union cavalrymen under the leadership of General Thomas Howard Ruger, the artist's second cousin. The family is transported to Vicksburg, Mississippi.

c. 1866-1874 Donoho and his mother settle in Washington, D.C., residing at 1332 I Street, N.W. He attends the Emerson Institute, an elite preparatory school for young men.

1874-1876 Studies at the State Normal School in Millersville, Pennsylvania.

1876-1877 Returns to Washington and is employed as a draughtsman by the Office of the United States Architect. Studies painting with local artists and possibly noted landscape painter, Robert Swain Gifford. Admires work of Jervis McEntee when it is exhibited in Washington.

1878 Summer and fall spent painting in the Catskills. In November Donoho moves to New York and enrolls at the Art Students League. Studies composition with Walter Shirlaw and painting with William Merritt Chase. Resumes sessions with Gifford at the Cooper Union School.

1879 Embarks for Paris in the fall. Registers at the Académie Julian with which he remains affiliated until 1887. Receives instruction from Gustave-Rodolphe Boulanger, Jules-Joseph Lefebvre, Adolphe-William Bouguereau and Tony Robert-Fleury. At the Julian meets American artists Kenyon Cox, Willard Metcalf, John Twachtman, Alexander Harrison, Frank Benson and Edmund Tarbell.

1880 Works in the ateliers of the Académie Julian throughout the fall and winter. Summers in the countryside near the forest of Fontainebleau. Fills sketchbooks with scenes of

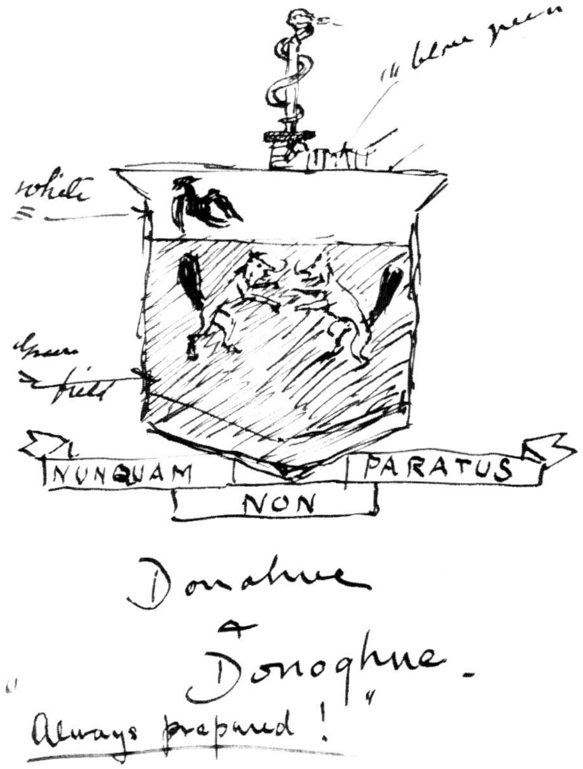

FIGURE 19.
Escutcheon, Donoho and Donoghue, n.d., ink on paper. Gaines Ruger Donoho Papers, Archives of American Art, Smithsonian Institution, Washington, D.C. Gift of John R. Hopkins. Drawing sent to Donoho by an unknown friend. Divided into color fields by the written designations "white," "blue-green" and "green-field" perhaps to describe the coloring of the shield or as a reference to the artist's palette.

Barbizon and Grez-sur-Loing. Develops contacts with Anglo-American art community at Grez.

1881 *The Edge of the Forest,* a Barbizon-inspired landscape, selected for the Paris Salon. Salon records list the artist's address as 5 rue Scribe, Paris.

1882 *La Marcellerie* and *La Garenne* exhibited at Paris Salon. Critical acclaim for *La Marcellerie* when shown in the United States at the Annual Exhibition of the Pennsylvania Academy of the Fine Arts in Philadelphia. Donoho joins the Society of American Artists.

1883 *Bad Pasture* and *Primroses* accepted for the Paris Salon and receive favorable reviews in the American art press. *La Marcellerie* shown in New York at the National Academy of Design and the Society of American Artists.

1884 The monumental *Shepherd* shown at the Paris Salon.

1885 Paris Salon entries include *Woman in the Woods.* Donoho awarded a prize for *The Edge of the Forest* at the International Cotton Exposition, New Orleans.

1886 *Self-Portrait* and *Faggot Gatherers* accepted by Paris Salon. Childe Hassam arrives in Paris and establishes friendship with Donoho.

1887 Returns to New York. Rents a studio at 146 West 55th Street.

1888 *Self-Portrait* and *Night* exhibited at the Society of American Artists. *The New Moon* and *November Woods* selected for National Academy of Design show.

1889 Awarded a silver medal at the Paris Universal Exposition for *La Marcellerie.* Joins the Lotus Players Club.

1890-1891 Moves to East Hampton, Long Island. Purchases large tract of land on Egypt Lane near the end of the village.

1892 Receives the Webb Prize from the Society of American Artists.

1893 Honorable Mention at the Columbian Exposition, Chicago, for *La Marcellerie* and *Explorers.*

1894 Marries Matilda Ackley of Philadelphia on April 13 in New York.

1895-1898 Maintains New York studio at 130 West 57th Street but curtails exhibition activity.

1898 Introduces Hassam to East Hampton. Under Hassam's influence, begins to experiment with the highly-keyed palette and short, choppy brushstroke of the Impressionist style, particularly in garden scenes.

1900-1901 Travels to Venice, Italy, and Marlotte and Pont Aven, France. Records these locales in dark, tonal landscapes. In East Hampton begins to paint the Woodhouse Water Gardens created in 1901.

1911 *A Garden* wins an Honorable Mention at the Carnegie Institute Annual Exhibition in Pittsburgh.

1913 *Self-Portrait* and *A Garden* exhibited at the Armory Show in New York.

1915 Receives a gold medal at the Panama-Pacific International Exposition, San Francisco for *A Garden.*

1916 Donoho dies June 28 in East Hampton. In November, Hassam organizes memorial exhibition at the Macbeth Gallery in New York. *Wind Flowers* purchased by J. Alden Weir for The Metropolitan Museum of Art.

1917 The Albright Art Gallery, Buffalo presents a Donoho exhibition.

Bibliography

Bermingham, Peter. *American Art in the Barbizon Mood.* Washington, D.C.: National Collection of Fine Arts, Smithsonian Institution Press, 1975.

Blaugrund, Annette, Ed. *Paris 1889: American Artists at the Universal Exposition.* Philadelphia: Pennsylvania Academy of the Fine Arts in association with Harry N. Abrams, Inc., 1989.

Braff, Phyllis. *Artists and East Hampton: A 100 Year Perspective.* East Hampton, New York: Guild Hall Museum, 1976.

Cameron, Katharine. *East Hampton: The 19th-Century Artist's Paradise.* Exhibition Catalogue. East Hampton, New York: Guild Hall Museum, 1991.

Catalogue of an Exhibition of Paintings by Ruger Donoho. Buffalo: Albright Art Gallery, 1917.

Champa, Kermit S. *The Rise of Landscape Painting in France: Corot to Monet.* Manchester, New Hampshire: The Currier Gallery of Art, 1991.

Fink, Lois Marie. *American Art at the Nineteenth-Century Paris Salons.* Cambridge: Cambridge University Press, 1990.

——— and Joshua Taylor. *Academy: The Academic Tradition in American Art.* Chicago and London: The University of Chicago Press, 1978.

Gerdts, William. *Art Across America.* New York: Abbeville Press, 1991.

Hassam, Childe. *Memorial Exhibition: Paintings by the Late Ruger Donoho.* Exhibition Catalogue. New York: Macbeth Gallery, 1916.

———. "Interview" (1927). De Witt McClellan Lockman Papers, Archives of American Art, Smithsonian Institution.

Isham, Samuel and Royal Cortissoz. *The History of American Painting.* New York: Macmillan, 1944.

Kurtz, Charles. *Illustrated Art Notes Upon the Fifty-Eighth Annual Exhibition of the National Academy of Design.* New York: National Academy of Design, 1883.

Langren, Marchel E. *Years of Art: The Story of the Art Students League of New York.* New York: Art Students League, 1940.

Meyers, Julia R. "The American Expatriate Painters of the French Peasantry, 1863-1893." Ph.D. Dissertation. University of Maryland, 1989.

Minty, Nancy. *Lyrical Visions: Turn-of-the-Century American Paintings from the Art Gallery of Ontario.* Toronto: Musée des

Beaux-Arts de l'Ontario, 1991.

Paris Salon: Explication des Oeuvrages de Peinture. Paris, 1881-1887.

Pisano, Ronald. *Long Island Landscape Painting, 1820-1920.* Boston: Little, Brown and Co., 1985.

———. *G. Ruger Donoho (1857-1916), A Retrospective Exhibition.* Exhibition Catalogue. New York: Hirschl & Adler Galleries, 1977.

Spassky, Natalie, et al. *American Paintings in The Metropolitan Museum of Art,* Vol. 2. New York: Metropolitan Museum of Art, 1985.

Weinberg, H. Barbara. *The Lure of Paris: Nineteenth-Century American Painters and Their French Teachers.* New York: Abbeville Press, 1991.

Exhibition Checklist

All dimensions are given in inches; height precedes width.

Barbizon, May, 1880
graphite on paper
8 ¾ x 17
Collection of Dr. Nancy Burrow and Dr. Kenneth Williams, Brandon, Mississippi

Forge, Fleury /study (verso), 1880
graphite on paper
10 ¼ x 13 ½
Collection of Mr. and Mrs. Davenport Mosby, Jackson, Mississippi

Millet's House, Barbizon, 1880
graphite on paper
10 ¼ x 13 ½
Collection of Dr. Nancy Burrow and Dr. Kenneth Williams, Brandon, Mississippi

Barbizon, June, c. 1880
graphite on paper
10 ⅛ x 13 ½
Collection of Dr. Nancy Burrow and Dr. Kenneth Williams, Brandon, Mississippi

Birches, 1881
graphite on paper
13 ¼ x 9 ⅞
Collection of Mr. and Mrs. Charles E. Carmichael, Jackson, Mississippi

Fleury, 1881
graphite on paper
10 ¼ x 13 ¾
Collection of Dr. Nancy Burrow and Dr. Kenneth Williams, Brandon, Mississippi

Forge, 1881
graphite on paper
13 ½ x 10 ¼
Collection of Mississippi Museum of Art, Jackson
Gift of Gallery Guild
1979.002

Grove, 1881
graphite on paper
8 ⅞ x 11 ⅞
Collection of Mr. and Mrs. Holmes S. Adams, Jackson, Mississippi

Churchyard, c. 1881
graphite on paper
10 ¼ x 13 ½
Collection of Mississippi Museum of Art, Jackson
Gift of Gallery Guild
1979.003

Landscape, c. 1881
graphite on paper
10 ¼ x 13 ¾
Collection of Mr. and Mrs. Holmes S. Adams and Mr. and Mrs. Harry M. Walker, Jackson, Mississippi

North West Knoll, c. 1881
graphite on paper
9 ¾ x 13 ½
Collection of Mississippi Museum of Art, Jackson
Gift of Alexander L. and Helena S. Nyerges
1989.001

Shepherd, 1884
oil on canvas
71 ⅜ x 47 ½
Collection of National Museum of American Art, Smithsonian Institution, Washington, D.C.
Gift of John R. Hopkins
1975.114

Self-Portrait, 1886
oil on canvas
24 ¾ x 19 ⅝
Collection of Mississippi Museum of Art, Jackson
Gift of Gallery Guild
1979.001

East Hampton Garden, c. 1890
oil on canvas
14 x 24
Collection of The Museums at Stony Brook, New York
Museum Purchase, 1989
89.14

Study of Sheep in Woods, East Hampton, c. 1890
oil on canvas
25 ¼ x 30
Collection of Mississippi Museum of Art, Jackson
Gift of Dr. and Mrs. Beckett Howorth, by exchange
1992.027

Trees of Heaven No. 2, c. 1890
oil on canvas
25 x 30
Collection of James J. Shields, New York, New York

Sheep, Late Afternoon, 1891
oil on canvas
24 x 44
Collection of Greenville County Museum of Art, South Carolina

Purchase, with funds from Mr. and Mrs. Christie C. Prevost
85.21.11

Drawing for Presidential banner in support of Theodore Roosevelt, 1892
watercolor, ink and graphite on paper
11 x 7 ⅞
Collection of East Hampton Library, Long Island Collection, New York

Egypt Beach in the Moonlight, c. 1898-1899
oil on canvas
16 x 30
Collection of Dan Flavin, Wainscott, New York

Old Hook Mill at Night, c. 1898-1899
oil on canvas
16 x 30
Collection of Dan Flavin, Wainscott, New York

Summer Night, c. 1898-1899
oil on canvas
20 x 24
Collection of James J. Shields, New York, New York

Entrance to John Howard Payne House, c. 1899
charcoal on paper
12 x 9 ⅝
Collection of Dan Flavin, Wainscott, New York

Home Sweet Home, c. 1899
oil on canvas
14 x 24
Collection of The Parrish Art Museum, Southampton, New York
Gift of Five Hopkins Brothers and Sisters
1977.2

Moonlight, Mills at Pont Aven, c. 1900
oil on canvas
30 x 36
Collection of High Museum of Art, Atlanta, Georgia
Purchase
31.6

Storm Over Loing Valley, 1902
oil on canvas
45 x 67 ½
Collection of Greenville County Museum of Art, South Carolina
Purchase, with assistance of (by exchange) Mr. and Mrs. Mason Alexander, in memory of Mr. Alexander's uncle, Mr. William H. Gardner; Mrs. William O. (Carolyn C.) Ballentine; Mr. and Mrs. Bernard Bertland; Burr Galleries; Mr. Thomas K. Connor; A.L. DePersio; Hugo Dreyfuss; Ferdinand Roten Galleries; Albert Fried, Jr.; John F. Hard; Mrs. J.M. Holmes; Dr. Melvin S. Horowitz; Mr. and

Mrs. Arthur F. Magill; J.F. McCrindle; Leo McDonald; Dr. C.P. Meek; Kenneth D. Moskowitz; Mr. and Mrs. John L. Petty, Jr.; Richard B. Sarver; and Michael Todd
88.21.13
Shown at Greenville County Museum of Art only

Auratum Lilies, 1907
oil on canvas
24 x 20
Collection of May and Frederick Hill, New York, New York

Wet Snow, Marlotte, 1907
oil on canvas
20 x 24
Collection of Mr. and Mrs. Charles C. Mickel, Greenville, South Carolina

Auratum Lilies No. 5, c. 1907
oil on canvas
20 x 30
Collection of Mr. and Mrs. William Kehl, Greenville, South Carolina

A Garden, 1911
oil on canvas
30 x 36
Collection of Art Gallery of Ontario, Toronto, Canada
Gift of Canadian National Exhibition Association, 1965
97

Blossom Time, Right of Path, Marlotte, c. 1911
oil on canvas
24 x 20
Collection of Mississippi Museum of Art, Jackson
Gift of Mrs. Velma Jernigan Rodgers
1981.272

Late Afternoon Winter, c. 1911
oil on canvas
30 x 36
Collection of New Orleans Museum of Art, Louisiana
Purchase, with funds from Major Benjamin Morgan Harrod Fund
30.1

Wind Flowers, 1912
oil on canvas
30 x 36
Collection of The Metropolitan Museum of Art, New York, New York
Rogers Fund, 1917
17.36

The Garden Steps, c. 1913
oil on canvas
15 ⅛ x 18 ⅛
Collection of Mississippi Museum of Art, Jackson
Gift of W.E. Walker Foundation
1978.036

Mississippi Museum of Art Staff

Linda S. Sullivan, *Executive Director*
Nina Moss, *Assistant to the Director*

ADMINISTRATIVE

Kimber Camper, *Security Staff*
Donnell Collier, *Security Staff*
Calvin Ellis, *Security Staff*
Michele Harris, *Director of Finance and Administration*
Pam Kinsey, *Museum Store Manager*
Emmanuel Madiebo, *Security Staff*
Anand Michael, *Chief of Security*
Julie Benson Norris, *Office Manager*
Julia Stewart, *Security Staff*

CURATORIAL

René Paul Barilleaux, *Director of Exhibitions and Collections/Chief Curator*
Sabrina Comola, *Director/Associate Curator, Corporate Art Program*
Melvin Johnson, *Associate Preparator*
L.C. Tucker, Jr., *Chief Preparator*
Beth Warren Turnage, *Assistant Curator/Registrar*

DEVELOPMENT

Elizabeth Martin Brister, *Director of Development*
Timothy Hedgepeth, *Public Relations and Membership Specialist*
Jean Weiss, *Manager of Membership Relations*
Andrea Wissner, *Manager of Marketing and Public Relations*

EDUCATION

Lisa McAnulty Avra, *Director of Education and Public Programs*
Sally Spencer, *Education Specialist for Youth and Academic Programs*

Photography Credits

FIGURES

1, 8, 9, 10, 11, 13, 14, 15, 16, 19–Archives of American Art, Smithsonian Institution

2, 3, 4, 5, 6, 7–James Patterson

12–The Brooklyn Museum

17–East Hampton Library

18–Guild Hall Museum

PLATES

1–National Museum of American Art, Smithsonian Institution

2–Williams & Williams, Inc.

3–The Museums at Stony Brook

4, 13, 16–Mississippi Museum of Art

5, 8–Edward Watkins

6, 11–Blake Praytor Photographer Inc.

7–Gary J. Mamay

9–High Museum of Art

10–Arthur Vitoli, Helga Photography

12–Carlo Catenazzi, Art Gallery of Ontario

14–New Orleans Museum of Art

15–The Metropolitan Museum of Art